RELATIVE GOOD

RELATIVE GOOD

DAVID GOW

Relative Good
first published 2012 by
Scirocco Drama
An imprint of J. Gordon Shillingford Publishing Inc.

Scirocco Drama Editor: Glenda MacFarlane
Cover design by Terry Gallagher / Doowah Design Inc.
Author photo by L. Kalo Gow
Printed and bound in Canada on 100% post-consumer recycled paper.

We acknowledge the financial support of the Manitoba Arts Council and The Canada Council for the Arts for our publishing program.

Library and Archives Canada Cataloguing in Publication

Gow, David, 1964-
Relative good / David Gow.

A play.
ISBN 978-1-897289-82-2

I. Title.

PS8563.O877R44 2012 C812'.54 C2012-904702-3

J. Gordon Shillingford Publishing
P.O. Box 86, RPO Corydon Avenue, Winnipeg, MB Canada R3M 3S3

For L. Kalo Gow
XV

Setting

In the premiere production, September 2005, the set was made largely of glass (plexi) with black metal and stainless steel. Corridors made of bowed glass created a funhouse effect and a central interrogation area doubled as Laila's living room. Often the actors not present in scenes, most particularly Laila, remained onstage and witnessed the events of the scenes. The action of the play was virtually continuous.

Characters

Mohammed El Rafi	A Syrian born Canadian citizen, thirty-five years old. A Muslim by ancestry, not observant. An engineer working in the field of hydrogen combustion. Intelligent, kind, not heroic or stoic. Speaks carefully and in a measured way.
Claire Hopkins	Canadian born and raised, from Surrey, New Brunswick, in her late twenties to early thirties. Likely grew up with United Church of Canada. A lawyer, top of her class. Without cynicism, but not naïve. Working in diplomatic field to try to achieve her goal of public service. Warm, but not effusive. Confident enough in herself to rock the boat quite hard.
Laila El Rafi	Canadian born and raised woman. Thirties. Muslim by ancestry, not observant. Educated, former teacher who has been at home full time with children in recent years. Intelligent, warm, expressive—she is however unused to taking a public position and making all the decisions for her family.
Jenkins	American born and raised. No discernible regional accent. In his late thirties. University educated Department of Homeland Security agent. Hard edged, very confident, though not overtly arrogant. No doubts that he is doing the right thing for his country. Unconcerned with courtesies that are afforded non-nationals in times of peace. Actor also doubles as waiter in Hodge scene.

The following four roles are played by one actor:

Customs Guard	American born and raised. Late forties, career Port Authority worker. Doing his job.
Terry Johnston	Johnston, sixty-five years old, is Claire's area supervisor at the Canadian Consul in New York. He has worked for decades in public service and is moments away from retirement. He can see his deck chair calling, with a gin and tonic on its arm and this guides his moves. He's concerned with the situation Claire presents him with, but long ago realised he is not the author of history or law.
Hodge	Sixty-three years old, a long-time career diplomatic corps type. A slight mid-Atlantic sound that would be at home in any capital or large city. Slightly effeminate, or perhaps just cultured. Hodge has more than a little power and enjoys exercising it. He is used to quick capitulation from underlings.
Barbara Murielle	The Canadian Consul in New York, a former media darling who has authored many books on gardening. Ms. Murielle adores her new job and is adored in it; unlike a traditional diplomat, she sees interpreting American realities to Canadians as her role instead of the inverse.
Voices on Public Address Systems:	Flight Attendant, Airport Security

Production History

The world premiere of *Relative Good* was produced by Great Canadian Theatre Company in Ottawa. It opened on September 6, 2005, with the following cast:

LAILA EL RAFFI .... Dalal Badr

CLAIRE HOPKINS .... Mary Ellis

MOHAMMED EL RAFFI .... Sam Kalilieh

TERRY / HODGE / MURIELLE .... Paul Rainville

JENKINS .... Richard Zeppieri

Directed by Michael Shamata

Set and Costume Design by John Ferguson

Lighting Design by Jock Munro

Lighting Operator: Jon Alexander

Sound Operator: Jon Carter

Wardrobe and Props: Sarah Freely

Stage Manager: Kevin Waghorn

Apprentice Stage Manager: Samira Rose

Relative Good was first produced as a radio play for CBC Radio.

David Gow

David Gow is the author of six full-length stage plays, and an award-winning internationally distributed featured film, *Steel Toes,* which Gow co-directed, starring Academy Award nominee David Strathairn. A number of awards for the film included Best Feature Film at The Beverly Hills Film Festival and Best Screenplay at Methodfest, Los Angeles. His plays have seen productions across Canada at many of Canada's most prestigious theatres (Montréal, Toronto, Vancouver, Edmonton), across the United States and, increasingly, around the world. In one recent theatre season Gow's work was seen in London, U.K., New York City, Berlin, Jerusalem, Te-Aviv, Montreal, and a number of other cities in Canada and the U.S. David's number of stand alone stage productions have crossed over the threshold of a hundred in the past decade, and the German translation of his play *Cherry Docs,* with Vaganten Buhne, played in repertoire for over six years in Berlin. At the same time, a number of productions in Poland have run in repertoire for over seven years.

Relative Good was staged in New York City in 2007 with the title *Arrivals* by Weisberger Theatre Group and the Bank Street Theatre. His most recent play *Wake of the Bones,* a musical about the discovery of the Irish immigrants mass grave in Montreal, premiered in 2010 at the Hudson Village Theatre in Hudson, QC. Other plays by Gow include *Bea's Niece, The Friedman Family Fortune, The Flight of Peter Pumpkin-eater* aka *Spout,* a one-man show. Gow holds an MFA in theatre / playwrighting from York University, Toronto.

Prologue

The sound of large passenger jets, passing directly above us and landing. The scream and whine of the turbine engines mixing with the whiffling of air brushing against the aluminium airframes, the skin of the craft. A number of passes directly overhead, then we hear as from inside a plane the sound of landing gear descending then hitting the tarmac with a clunk, and the slight screech of tires. The turbines reversing in a rush to slow the craft.

A female flight attendant's voice over a plane's P.A. system.

Ladies and gentleman, we have just landed in New York City, the temperature is 18 degrees under sunny skies. *Mesdames et messieurs, nous sommes arrivée a New York, il fait beau et dix huit.* Kindly remain seated…

Scene One

Morning, New York City, Customs concourse in JFK airport. MO is waiting to be called forward to a kiosk manned by a CUSTOMS GUARD.

P.A. VOICE: Homeland Security in compliance with the Patriot Act requires that you keep all baggage with you and be prepared to be searched at any time.

We hear chimes and beeps made by electronic gear used for security. Establish, then build the dull roar of five hundred people, chatting in a subdued manner, talking on cell phones, or silent: all waiting to be processed at the customs concourse of JFK airport. The talking mounts and the sound becomes almost a wall, a waterfall's roar. Then, silence.

CUSTOMS GUARD: *(Voice raised somewhat, impatient.)* You were born where?

MO: Syria.

CUSTOMS GUARD: You were born there.

MO: Yes, sir.

CUSTOMS GUARD: And you're currently a citizen of?

MO: Canada.

CUSTOMS GUARD: Since?

MO: Always.

CUSTOMS GUARD: And this is your name since birth, Mohammed El Rafi?

MO: Yes, but everyone calls me Mo.

CUSTOMS GUARD: You were born in Syria?

MO: Yes.

CUSTOMS GUARD: You sound pretty much Canadian.

MO: My Mother's from North Bay, originally.

CUSTOMS GUARD: Where's that?

MO: Very far North.

CUSTOMS GUARD: Near Russia?

MO: No, not so far North as that.

CUSTOMS GUARD: OK, you stay here. Don't move at all. I have to speak with the Port Director…

MO: Yes, sir.

CUSTOMS GUARD: Stand perfectly still, I'll be right back.

Yes.

MO reaches into his pocket, retrieves a cell phone which he flips open and turns on, dials.

Hello, Jan Peters. *(Pause.)* I could be a little late this morning. Delay at the airport; security… Something's up here, you should see the security, they're coming my way—they're, oh no…they're coming towards me…

We see MO arrested at gunpoint, walked into interrogation room.

Scene Two

Morning, New York City, an interrogation room in the customs area.

MO: I'm a Canadian citizen.

JENKINS: So?

MO: Under the Canadian Constituti–

JENKINS: You're not in Canada.

MO: Under the American Const—

JENKINS: You're not under the American Constitution, you're not in America.

MO: Where am I?

JENKINS: A port.

MO: Which is?

JENKINS: A port of entry. You haven't entered America, yet.

MO: Then where…?

JENKINS: Nowhere.

MO: I would ask to return to Canada.

JENKINS: You're under arrest by American Port Authority. We need to question you…

MO: On the subject of hydrogen combustion?

JENKINS: Among other things.

MO: Such as?

JENKINS: The position of Muslim people on certain issues.

MO: I can't speak for the Muslim people.

JENKINS: You're evading.

MO: I'm not.

JENKINS: You've travelled extensively in the Middle East.

MO: On business.

JENKINS: Whose business?

MO: Mine, for my employer.

JENKINS: And your knowledge from those travels as well as your cultural…your religious orientation is critically important to us.

MO: Look, it is my constitutional right…

JENKINS: Not here. We'd like you to volunteer to be questioned in Syria.

MO: Questioned in Syria?

JENKINS: Yes.

MO: No. Absolutely not.

JENKINS: Cooperation would make this less of an ordeal. *(Pause.)* You were born there.

MO: My father, a Canadian citizen, did business in Syria. That's why we were there.

JENKINS: Oh yes, we know all about that. He was also born there.

MO: I'm a citizen of Canada.

JENKINS: So you say. *(Pause.)* You're a Syrian born Muslim…

MO: I'd like to see a lawyer, a consular representative…

JENKINS: So you've requested, a number of times. *(Short pause.)* It would be for the good of your country, my country—our countries, if you would volunteer to go to Syria.

MO: I'm not going to.

JENKINS: *(Pause.)* You have children. *(Silence.)* For their good.

MO: …My children.

JENKINS: For the whole society—

Silence.

MO: No.

JENKINS: I'm asking again, for the good of the homeland.

Silence.

MO: Absolutely not.

JENKINS: You're not interested in helping us out?

MO: I did not say that.

JENKINS: What's the difference?

MO: …I'm from Canada.

JENKINS: I'm telling you that is not relevant here. We don't care.

MO: What do you want?

JENKINS: Cooperation.

MO: I…I…do have rights…

JENKINS: Very few. Almost none here. We have American citizens under arrest on National Security Certificates—less rights than you… I want you to make a choice, a moral choice for good. For security.

MO: I'm not going to Syria.

JENKINS: What makes you think you have that choice.

MO: What are we talking about, what do you want to know?

JENKINS: Everything, everything you know. In detail.

MO: How long will this take?

JENKINS: Less time with your co-operation. This is why you need to go to Syria. They have all the relevant information. It would take less time…

Silence.

I know that the idea of Syria is frightening. I want you to think of your children, think about their safety, their enjoyment of life.

Scene Three

The following morning. Airport, New York City, a hallway off the interrogation room. CLAIRE crosses the stage through corridors with JENKINS.

CLAIRE: Is he in there?

JENKINS: Ms. Hopkins, we're waiting for word. Your consulate briefed you?

CLAIRE: I must speak with him.

JENKINS: We're waiting for word.

CLAIRE: From?

JENKINS: Higher up.

CLAIRE: From whom?

JENKINS: Those above me.

CLAIRE: And you are?

JENKINS: Special Agent Jenkins, Homeland Security— You can see my name on my ID tag, number's there too. I can't answer anything else till I get a "clear."

Short silence.

CLAIRE: How long has he been here.

JENKINS: Less than twenty four hours.

CLAIRE: A day. *(Pause.)* International law, and custom requires that a Canadian citizen be returned to Canada if refused entry.

JENKINS: I'm not going to argue with you, Ma'am. The man was born in Syria. That makes him first and foremost a Syrian national.

CLAIRE:. He's a citizen of Canada. I demand to see him.

JENKINS: Demand?

CLAIRE: I do.

JENKINS: Have you talked to your superiors? We have documents coming in on this guy from CSIS…

CLAIRE: I'll call my office, this should be an open and shut case.

JENKINS: It's not. *(On cell phone.)* Yes, sir. Yes, sir. No, sir. I understand. Visual confirmation of well being, yes sir. *(Pause.)* I can give you a couple of moments with the detainee.

CLAIRE: Moments?

JENKINS: It's the best I can do, for now.

CLAIRE: I'll take that.

JENKINS: Come this way.

CLAIRE and JENKINS walking through a number of security doors with buzzers on them under the following.

If you weren't so quick to give terrorists citizenship…

CLAIRE: His mother's family's been in Canada since the potato famine in Ireland.

JENKINS: Look, his father is Syrian, and he was born in Syria.

Here he is. *(They enter the interrogation room.)* I'm taking off your blindfold; you have a visitor, Mr. El Rafi. This is Claire Hopkins, your…she's an attorney with the Canadian Consulate.

MO: Thank you for seeing me. I truly appreciate it.

CLAIRE: It's my pleasure. We'll do everything we can for you.

MO: That's comforting to hear.

CLAIRE: Are you being well treated?

MO: *(Avoiding this.)* Yes.

CLAIRE: Have you been fed?

MO: …Please, do whatever you can to get me on a plane, a bus back to Canada, nothing else matters.

CLAIRE: You're not feeding him.

JENKINS: This isn't a restaurant, he'll get something. That's all the time I can offer you for now.

MO: Please, tell my wife, to give my love to the children…

A very loud dull horn goes off, obliterating his words.

Scene Four

Continuous. Airport, New York City, a hallway off the interrogation room.

CLAIRE: Was the siren necessary?

JENKINS: He could be communicating some vital information through code.

CLAIRE: I'm amazed at your level of alert.

JENKINS: And we're amazed at how asleep you are as a nation. A safe harbour for terrorists, for terrorist fundraising, money laundering, drug trafficking. You give out passports like party favours. And we have to keep the continent safe, pay for an army… while you have socialist medicine.

CLAIRE: National health insurance…?

JENKINS: Socialized, nationalized… We have citizens dead because of your soft borders, your soft attitudes, lax laws, lack of concern. *(Pause.)* Couple of thousand dead in Toronto, you'd jump right to attention. This is your door I'm showing you out.

CLAIRE: Pearl Harbour. That's what it took to get America into World War II.

JENKINS: And we learned our lesson, since then we've been watching the world. Lotsa luck, I don't think you'll find this one business as usual.

CLAIRE: Thank you for your cooperation.

JENKINS: Why do you Canadians always say "thank you"? I don't work for you.

CLAIRE: I appreciate your assistance.

JENKINS: I'm doing my job. If I could do it and keep you out of this Port, I'd be happier.

CLAIRE: Well, thank you, again.

A brief pause and then, a door buzzes open, the sound of the airport's main concourse…

P.A. VOICE: Homeland Security in compliance with the Patriot Act requires that you report any suspicious behavior. Suspicion is the better part of caution, report any supicious bags or parcels left unattended.

Scene Five

Day. The Canadian Consulate, the office of JOHNSTON, CLAIRE's boss. Far off traffic and big city sounds.

CLAIRE: So that's the position, sir?

JOHNSTON: It might very well appear that way; but I don't know if we would be advised to call it a position.

CLAIRE: …Would you call it a directive?

JOHNSTON: Not really…

CLAIRE: But it's the way that it is?

JOHNSTON: Certainly is.

CLAIRE: …So it is a…defining aspect of this particular situation…?

JOHNSTON: For now.

CLAIRE: This flies in the face of all past precedent and practice, sir.

JOHNSTON: I wouldn't go that far.

CLAIRE: Why not, sir?

JOHNSTON: You needn't call me sir, Claire.

CLAIRE: Very well, Mr. Johnston.

JOHNSTON: Johnston is fine. *(Pause.)* Have I shown you Claire, the photo of my cottage? *(He takes a photo from his breast pocket and shows it to CLAIRE.)* I've had it completely winterized. It's ready to live in the minute I retire, I'm counting the days… It's a five minute drive to the nearest store…

CLAIRE: It's lovely, and yes you've shown it to me before. *(Pause.)* Johnston, we've got a citizen, half shitting himself they're going to pack him off to Syria like a lobster in a box…

JOHNSTON: …Oh now… *(JOHNSTON continues to gaze at the photo of his cottage.)*

CLAIRE: That is exactly what is going on. He was born there, has not done military service there, could be subject to torture there, unlimited detention.

JOHNSTON: The world has changed since nine eleven…

CLAIRE: From anything other than a hard right, skip that, totalitarian point of view, we're giving them the victory…

JOHNSTON: …Them?

CLAIRE: …ugh.

JOHNSTON: Claire, my dear, you're upset, the sight of a man blindfolded, the horrible pictures everyone saw, the whole notion of sexual humiliation it conjures up.

CLAIRE: *(She notices his odd comment and decides to ignore it.)* We are giving them the victory.

JOHNSTON: The…"right wing people"…

CLAIRE: The terrorists. *(Pause.)* Thousands were killed, and I can't say, granted, but I do know about it, did see it, was here…but we are giving the terrorists the victory if we as a society suspend our own basic rights…

Silence.

JOHNSTON: Claire. *(Pause.)* One, this man is not an American and he is in America as are we outside of these doors… Or rather, he's being detained by Americans. Two, were he an American, he could find himself in the very same situation or worse. Three, the laws have already changed and as a liberal—and of course I mean that not in the party sense—but as a liberal— if you haven't noticed that—your head's so far in the sand you must be breathing through your rear quarters. In Canada, too. Sweeping changes. Sweeping. Alright? If you can't adjust, you could ask to be re-assigned…back home.

CLAIRE: Have they got anything on this guy, anything at all?

JOHNSTON: One of the people he was associated with in his youth is in detention currently in Syria.

CLAIRE: Is that a…? Is that a fact. Look, Johnston. The thing is, I want him out of there. He's a citizen—and it's my job, it's my docket—you know… I'm supposed to look after this kind of thing—and get him—put him in the best position I can, as a visiting Canadian…

JOHNSTON: They're taking the position he's not visiting, that he's detained in the Port.

CLAIRE: OK, well—he's detained. He is a citizen.

JOHNSTON: Of Canada, yes. The Syrians also would see him as a citizen.

CLAIRE: Does he carry a Syrian passport?

JOHNSTON: No, but he's travelled all over the Middle East, all of his life. He works with hydrogen combustion. This is not an average Joe. An average situation.

CLAIRE: And the position, sorry, the situation he's in, where the Consulate is concerned is…

JOHNSTON: Not good, from his standpoint. *(Pause.)* The fellow is being detained, not on my authority or yours. He is being detained by the Director of the Port and the Department of Homeland Security, and, he's not exactly in America…

CLAIRE: That's the Consulate's position?

JOHNSTON: That's the situation. The situation he finds himself in.

CLAIRE: I'll speak with the Vice Consul.

JOHNSTON: And that, Claire was not my idea.

CLAIRE: *(Smiling almost through her teeth.)* Johnston, Mr. Johnston, sir, you can rest assured that I leave not this meeting with the thought that you have given me any idea at all…

JOHNSTON: *(Pause.)* Thank you. *(Stopping her.)* Claire. *(Pause.)* I have a couple of weeks left, a comfortable little place in the Thousand Islands, winters in Arizona. I've worked forty-five years. I'm already anticipating the quiet.

CLAIRE: The Thousand Islands… Isn't that where there's a community association petitioning to have jet flight paths kept out of the area…

JOHNSTON: Yes, that's right. …I'm not involved in that.

CLAIRE: …For the male kingfisher, he's sensitive to sound and won't mate when jets are in the area…?

JOHNSTON: That's correct, again, I'm uninvolved…

CLAIRE: Thank you, Johnston.

Scene Six

End of the day. Airport, New York City, the interrogation room.

MO: I have told you a hundred times. I am not a terrorist, I am not an extremist, I am not a religious fundamentalist, nor fanatic.

JENKINS: I've heard it a hundred times…

MO: What?

JENKINS: Are you getting anywhere?

MO: No.

JENKINS: Why don't you try something else…

MO: Like…?

JENKINS: Tell us something new.

MO: I am telling you the truth.

JENKINS: As you see it.

MO: It is the truth. The truth is not an act of negotiation.

JENKINS: Your truth is suspect; automatically suspect.

MO: Because of my national origin.

JENKINS: That's one point.

MO: And my family's religious background…?

JENKINS: You fit a certain profile, there are many other factors involved. For example, your detailed knowledge of hydrogen combustion.

MO: My detailed knowledge is no secret. Everything that I know has come from somewhere… I have not created any truly major breakthroughs or revelations in this field. I am no Einstein, sadly…

JENKINS: Bullshit. You're dealing with explosive materials.

MO: We're trying to power cars with it, generating stations. It would lessen our reliance on oil, this is not a threat to you, it's only to your benefit. I am working with your government on this…

JENKINS: Last year you were in Egypt.

MO: Yes.

JENKINS: On business?

MO: I went to see my Grandfather, he's almost a hundred.

JENKINS: Was that business?

MO: No. It was personal.

JENKINS: You've described your trips as business trips, but last year you went to Egypt on a personal trip.

MO: It's not illegal to go to Egypt, is it?

JENKINS: It's part of your profile, part of what is bringing you scrutiny.

MO: I took no work materials with me whatsoever, not even a laptop. I was very careful.

JENKINS: Careful, why?

MO: Knowing that my area of work is in a sensitive— Is this about my work?

JENKINS: It's about everything. And it's about you in particular.

MO: A hundred times, I've told you I have nothing to hide.

JENKINS: Then why won't you agree go to Syria?

MO: In Syria, I am not a citizen in the normal sense, I've told you this… My family is not welcome there, I was born there but did not do military service there, as I am a Canadian and was living in Canada at that age… I would very likely be subject to torture there or possibly just disappear. Have you any concept…?

JENKINS: Thousands disappeared in this city in one day.

MO: I am sorry for your loss, very sorry. *(Pause.)* I had nothing to do with it.

JENKINS: You did, you did indeed.

MO: In what regard?

JENKINS: By virtue of your existence.

MO: How's—?

JENKINS: Assuming you are everything you say and nothing else. The innocent Muslims in this country hid the guilty.

MO: I did no such thing—

JENKINS: You did. Just by being here. You put a reasonable modern face on your people, which kept us from seeing the extremists—

MO: The man who bombed the federal building in Oklahoma. That man was American…

JENKINS: So; yes…

MO: That does not make all Americans bad, does it. Or, all people who have been in the military bad—he had been in the mili—

JENKINS: *(Raising his voice.)* Do you really expect me to go through all this with you over and over again. We do not want lessons from you or sermons. We want you to give us whatever information you have on extremists, on terrorists, on fundamentalist religious groups…

MO: …Look, I get up at six a.m. to see my kids ready for school… My wife drives them, I pick up a large coffee with cream at Tim Hortons.

JENKINS: *(Pause.)* …Who's that?

MO: That's a coffee chain, like Starbucks, but for regular people…

JENKINS: *(Pause.)* OK.

MO: Then I drive to work, checking my messages by cell phone… I work from about eight in the morning until at least seven p.m. Once in a while I see my children for supper… I work late, I work weekends.

I fly around the continent and sometimes the world… *(Pause.)* I haven't been to a mosque since I was a kid. My wife tells me she misses me and fears we are growing apart…this has been my life for many years. How much time do you think I have for encountering extremists and religious fundamentalists, let alone terrorists… *(Pause.)* I am run off my feet, just trying to live my life and do my work…

JENKINS: So, you deny any association with these groups.

MO: Yes, emphatically, yes, I do deny it as I have no association…

JENKINS: Then we are not getting anywhere. *(Pause.)* You are going to get put on a plane for Syria if this keeps up.

MO: If you want me to tell you something, confess to something, incriminate someone: tell me. I cannot guess what you are after…I haven't got the head for it.

JENKINS: *(Pause.)* We might be able to work with that…that's a thought.

Scene Seven

Early evening, a restaurant, New York City. Perhaps establish the tinkling and clinking of a nice high-end dining salon. Music; Upbeat, well played calm, cool jazz. VICE CONSUL HODGE and CLAIRE.

HODGE: Have you tried the fois gras here? It's quite *(Pause.)* respectable.

CLAIRE: No.

HODGE: Well. You must, I insist. I'm at the Met at eight, but I think we can have a snack, yes?

CLAIRE: I thank you for working me into your agenda

on such short notice, Mr. Vice Consul. It's a real situation we've got at the airport…

HODGE: Oh yes, it's very hot. I don't think I can talk about that.

CLAIRE: Respectfully sir, we have to talk about it. I need your instruction. I need it now.

HODGE: Vis a vis what?

CLAIRE: The matter we were discussing.

HODGE: We weren't discussing anything…

CLAIRE: We were discussing a Canadian citizen, being held here in New York…

HODGE: No. *(Irritated.)* I'm not speaking about some traveller in trouble with Customs. Too fine a set of details for me, just before an evening out. I don't know about it, do you hear me? *(Pause.)* You're from Surrey, New Brunswick, correct, dear?

CLAIRE: Yes, sir.

HODGE: A lot of real estate deals down there?

CLAIRE: I suppose so, yes sir.

HODGE: Do you like real estate law?

CLAIRE: I specialised in international law, top of my class, sir.

HODGE: Of course, course. We're all highly qualified. Now.

CLAIRE: Yes. *(Pause.)* Real estate law?

HODGE: Do you want to practise it?

CLAIRE: I'd prefer to be here.

HODGE: Well. You might find it hard even to practise real estate law in Surrey if you can't play ball, if you can't face these tough realities.

CLAIRE: ...Are you threatening me, sir?

HODGE: Head of your class, figure it out. Well.

CLAIRE: This man needs our help.

HODGE: Well go ahead, suit yourself. I'm not discussing it. Next thing, there will be reporters calling.

CLAIRE: I am going to discuss this, I will be discussing this, and not just over drinks. If you refuse to discuss this, I will take this matter to the Consul herself.

HODGE: *(Just slightly under his voice.)* You are a pigheaded little bitch. *(Pause.)* I never said that. Got a fierce headache coming on, triggers inappropriate responses. How do feel about selling real estate? Of course there's a licensing process...

CLAIRE: Are you telling me, that I can't look after this citizen's needs?

HODGE: Not at all. Put him in an hotel. Send him to a nice show, get him an upgrade for his trip home—that's the sort of thing...

CLAIRE: He's in custody with a blindfold on. They're going to deport him to a country known for torturing detainees...

HODGE: No, no, no. I really have got an awful headache. A migraine in fact. It's a good thing I have a driver and a pool car tonight.

WAITER: I think you caught my eye, yes?

HODGE: Yes. What is this wine I'm drinking?

WAITER: It's what you ordered, sir. This is our Raven's Feather, Mountain Trumpeteer. It's a California, Rocky Mountain claret.

HODGE: I'll not have the Mountain Trumpet, I'll have any proper Barolo, from the Coalition Partner Country of Italy please, you pick…

WAITER: Right away, sir.

HODGE: Think about it. Think about what it would be like to answer phones and photocopy contracts at a real estate agency as a temp in your hometown, when no one else is available. At Christmas once a year. Oh, this pounding pounding…must have had sulphides… North American wine, even the best… screaming headache… Will you take my tickets for this evening?

CLAIRE: I'm working, doing my…doing my best to do my job. If you can get me fired for that, sir…

HODGE: I can indeed. I certainly can. Will I? This is a political situation, of import between our two great and shining nations.

CLAIRE: I agree. Good night, sir.

HODGE: Claire, think it over. Pumping gas at a small independent gas station. Big chain couldn't have a security risk…

CLAIRE: I will think, sir. Thank you so much. Goodnight.

Scene Eight

Evening, the airport, interrogation room.

CLAIRE: I can't say that it's going well.

MO: How long will it take?

CLAIRE: The problem is the laws have all changed. Sweeping changes. And while I've read them, the laws that is, they are so general, so broad, so…sweeping…

MO: Yes…?

CLAIRE: Well. Laws need to be interpreted, tested. Re-tested, appealed etc.

MO: While that's going on, what happens to me?

CLAIRE: The long and the short of it is they're not releasing you to Canadian authorities, nor are they willing to return you to Canada.

MO: *(Pause.)* Oh.

CLAIRE: Are you being fed?

MO: I was given some fast food burgers. I am not a stoic, in the face of threats, if physically intimidated.

CLAIRE: Are you being threatened?

MO: In Syria, my uncle was imprisoned for several years, he died in prison, no one knows how… My father's entire family could not find work with significant education, even when there was lots of work to be had… In Syria, as a Syrian born, I am required to have done military service. I have not done that service. *(Pause)* They don't need to threaten me too much, all they need to say is we're sending you to Syria and I am immediately in distress. My heart races, my palms sweat. I've already told them everything I know, which is nothing, on the subject of terrorism—aside from what I've picked up travelling and on CNN. *(Pause.)* I've tried to elucidate the various forms of Muslim practise and what the groups believe—who is more prone to see violence as a solution…

CLAIRE: …As a solution?

MO: Many Muslim peoples feel pressed, oppressed by the West, they feel in every instance driven from their territory…

CLAIRE: This is not your point of view…?

MO: I am not a practising Muslim and neither was my father. Interrogated, threatened, I can give some of the point of view in broad strokes… I have also said more about hydrogen technology than I think is permitted in certain agreements I have signed both with Canadian and US agencies. I wonder will I be in great trouble for that?

CLAIRE: You're speaking here with US agencies…

MO: Oh yes… *(Laughs.)* but perhaps not the same authority…? Perhaps…I am tired. What time is it?

CLAIRE: Nine p.m.

MO: Nine p.m. on what day?

CLAIRE: You were detained the day before yesterday. Tuesday. Today is Thursday.

MO: Oh. *(Pause.)* It seems so much longer. Did you speak to my wife?

CLAIRE: I left a message. I'll try her again tonight.

MO: Good.

CLAIRE: I'm going to speak with the Consul tomorrow…I hope.

MO: Thank you.

CLAIRE: You're welcome.

MO: I can see you are doing your best…I very much appreciate it. I do not want to speak of my family as that alarm…might go off again.

CLAIRE: I will give them all your love and best wishes.

MO: Yes, precisely, any way at all that that is expressed.

There's no code in it. I've always been a proud Canadian. I am as Canadian as you, I think? Well maybe not quite…well yes I am, aren't I? Do I have an accent?

CLAIRE: Not an accent, no. Not quite.

MO: But a certain something, an idiom. The son of an accent. The father has an accent and he has a trace, that's what I've heard people say—since kindergarten…

CLAIRE: Where did you grow up?

MO: N.D.G. in Montreal.

CLAIRE: N.D.G.?

MO: You don't think I'm a terrorist Ms. Hopkins? You haven't asked me directly.

CLAIRE: *(Pause.)* I've seen no evidence that you are anything other than what you say you are.

MO: Thank you. I have to admit I am very anxious, very tired.

CLAIRE: Have you slept much?

MO: I have not seen a clock or daylight since I arrived. So, I do not know when I have slept.

CLAIRE: I will speak with the Consul first thing in the morning…

MO: I thank you from the bottom of my heart for your caring and concern in my case. *(He begins to break down, possibly lapsing to anger.)* …I know that I am guiltless and that…I have worked for my country and this country too…I am considered one of the top in my field…I have given my heart and soul to my work, for the advancement of a…the betterment of our society…for a cleaner burning…

CLAIRE: I believe we should be able to do something for you.

MO: Do you? Do you really?

JENKINS: *(Entering.)* That's all the time I can give you…

MO: …Again I thank you.

CLAIRE: I'll do my very best for you. I promise.

Scene Nine

Night, a phone conversation between two women in their respective homes (or a car and a home).

CLAIRE: Hello Mrs. El Rafi…?

LAILA: Yes…hello? Who is this, please?

CLAIRE: My name is Claire Hopkins, I'm an attorney working at the Canadian Consulate in New York City. I deal with jurisdiction…I left you a message…

LAILA: Yes…?

CLAIRE: I've just seen your husband minutes ago.

LAILA: *(Pause.)* Is he alright?

CLAIRE: He's okay.

LAILA: I have not heard from him in two days.

CLAIRE: *(Pause.)* He's being detained by the American authorities at what we would call immigration.

LAILA: Detained…? Did you say detained?

CLAIRE: Yes, detained.

LAILA: What for? He works in new technology…

CLAIRE: Yes, I don't think that's the cause of his detention, specifically, though it may be related.

LAILA: Ms. Hopkins, did you say?

CLAIRE: Yes, or Claire is my name.

LAILA: Claire, what do you think is the cause of his detention.

CLAIRE: His background. Where he was born, his ancestry.

LAILA: I see. *(Pause.)* We are both very Canadian… Look, we don't follow any religion formally…

CLAIRE: He wants you to know he loves you very much.

Silence.

LAILA: When will they release him?

CLAIRE: I'm working on that.

LAILA: Should I come down there.

CLAIRE: NO. I would strongly advice against that. In fact I insist you not consider that. We may need you exactly where you are.

LAILA: I don't understand what's going on here. What do they think he is…?

CLAIRE: There's a possibility…I'm working against this, there's a possibility he could be deported to his country of birth.

LAILA: *(Pause.)*…Syria? *(Pause.)* Mo doesn't go to Syria, ever. He…uh he can't go there…are you sure you don't want me to come down there.

CLAIRE: I'm positive, Mrs. El Rafi. Please stay in Montreal. I will be in touch as soon as I have news. Yes?

LAILA: I understand. You can call at any hour…

CLAIRE: I'll stay in touch. You'll stay there? It's critical, you understand? It may be the only point of leverage we have, a family member in Canada.

LAILA: I understand.

CLAIRE: I'll call when I have news.

LAILA: Thank you, Claire.

Scene Ten

Day, the large office of the Canadian Consul.

BARBARA: *(Making a grand entrance.)* Claire.

CLAIRE: Madame Consul, it's good of you to see me on short notice. I've always enjoyed your books…your *Garden on a Balcony* in particular…

BARBARA: It's my pleasure, Claire. Call me Barbara.

CLAIRE: Very well. I was brought up that one calls one's seniors by their honorific or last name…

BARBARA: Where were you brought up, wait, east coast, correct?

CLAIRE: Correct.

BARBARA: Culture has shifted, Mores shift. Call me Barbara, but only if I say so, and not if you're in trouble…ha ha. There's a good deal of hypocrisy there. Actually puts people off balance guessing just what kind of terms they're on…

CLAIRE: Quite. *(Pause.)* So, I take it then I'm not in trouble.

BARBARA: No, no. Not quite trouble—however we will need to make some adjustments.

CLAIRE: Adjustments Ma'am? Uh Barbara. Barbara.

BARBARA: Yes?

CLAIRE: Adjustments. What might I adjust?

BARBARA: Well I wouldn't say your whole attitude, but damn near, Missy.

CLAIRE: Regarding?

BARBARA: There's an awkwardness with contemporary idiom that you need to lose right away, and I'm not just talking about the Ma'am, Sir, last name stuff.

CLAIRE: Very well…

BARBARA: You need to in every instance when referring to a port, an airport, immigration office—any large public facility to insert and keep it there, the word "secure" ahead of it. Use the word often and single it out.

CLAIRE: OK, I believe I could do that.

BARBARA: Not "border" "secure border."Not "airport," "secure airport." Give it a try: "Border."

CLAIRE: "Secure border."

BARBARA: "Airport."

CLAIRE: *(Laughing slightly.)* "Secure airport." How am I doing…?

BARBARA: You need to work at it. This is no joke. Every morning in the mirror, till it comes out naturally and confidently. "Industrial relations"…

CLAIRE: I will work at it…

BARBARA: Try "industrial relations"…

CLAIRE: *(Smiling.)* "Industrial relations", "secure industrial relations."

BARBARA: You've got to work at this until it's completely natural—or you will have trouble at every step here. OK?

CLAIRE: Yes, Ma'am.

BARBARA: Yes, "Barbara". *(Laughs, CLAIRE joins her.)* This seems silly but it is essential to master the idiom of the day and get it right or we stand out like a sore thumb as foreigners.

CLAIRE: Yes. I will work at it. *(Pause.)* I'm extremely concerned about our citizen's security.

BARBARA: *(Quite pleased to see a variation.)* Good, that a girl.

CLAIRE: Oh, no. I'm not trying right now…

BARBARA: It's coming very natural then. Good.

CLAIRE: Our citizen, Mohammed El Rafi, his "security".

BARBARA: Ah…I thought you meant citizens. I see, apostrophe. Yes, I'm aware of his case. It's the airport, the country here that we are guests in, that we are trying to assert is "secure," not Mr. El Rafi. Well wait a minute, I misspoke. We are concerned with Mr. El Rafi's "security" especially as it pertains to "homeland security."

CLAIRE: Yes. This is what I wanted to see you about.

BARBARA: Mr. El Rafi's security in relation to "security."

CLAIRE: Yes. I believe there's been a mistake. There seems to be no evidence against…

BARBARA: Oh We don't know that…

CLAIRE: There's nothing they've offered other than that he used as a reference another man who is also under suspicion.

BARBARA: Oh no. Quite wrong. There may be any amount of invisible evidence which might connect Mr. El Rafi to the pernicious roots and tubers of the international, subterranean, terrorist weed.

CLAIRE: And where is this evidence?

BARBARA: By law, they are not required to provide it.

CLAIRE: OK, but Madam Consul, Barbara…

BARBARA: Every morning in front of the mirror…

CLAIRE: Barbara, if you could meet him. His life's work is developing new technologies to lessen dependence on oil…

BARBARA: I knew it and you've just confirmed it…

CLAIRE: What's that?

BARBARA: You're too close to the "detainee," Mr. Whatsit?

CLAIRE: Mohammed El Rafi. Mo, his friends call him.

BARBARA: You are too close. He's married?

CLAIRE: Yes.

BARBARA: You?

CLAIRE: Not married.

BARBARA: You are?

CLAIRE: Unattached?

BARBARA: *(Lengthening the word.)* S-i-n-g-l-e. Sometimes it helps us recover power if we can give the proper name to a situation.

CLAIRE: …Well, yes, but that's not really relevant…

BARBARA: The American interrogator says he sees an empathy, a warmth, a…an inappropriate level of concern… whether that attraction—maternal or otherwise… it seems evident, even at this distance and without him in the room…

CLAIRE: Mr. El Rafi is a citizen…

BARBARA: Detained by American authorities in their secure airport.

CLAIRE: What about his "security" under our constitution and international law.

BARBARA: *(Pause.)* Weren't you a member of the young Progressive Conservatives, when we had such a thing. Your file says strong liberal tendencies.

CLAIRE: I "was" a member, as you say, when there was such a thing. Conservatives are allowed to support the constitution, as well as the Geneva Convention—

BARBARA: It's no damn good to call me Madam Consul, Ma'am, and then debate with me…

CLAIRE: I uh…

BARBARA: Listen to me, Claire, Ms. Hopkins, this is not a debating society. We are here to serve the common good of the Canadian people in relation to our very large and constant neighbour. "Relative good" actually sometimes is the objective, understood?

CLAIRE: I uh…am I not to look after Mr. El Rafi's rights as an individual?

BARBARA: Yes. As against the common good of two nations, you were to look after Mr. El Rafi…

CLAIRE: "Were"

BARBARA: Were. It's been suggested to me that you are overly involved in this case in a personal way, and speaking with you only confirms the matter for me.

CLAIRE: I beg to offer a different…

BARBARA: No. No, no.

CLAIRE: May I not offer to you, the other side of this…

BARBARA: As I have said, Claire, this is not a debating society, "security" matters of "international security" are at stake here… You will no longer be working on the case of one Mr. El Rafi.

CLAIRE: No longer…I've only just begun…I promised.

BARBARA: Do you understand, Claire? Finished.

Silence.

CLAIRE: Is that your final position?

BARBARA: Irrevocably; yes.

Pause.

CLAIRE: I am forced then, under the circumstances, Barbara, Madam Consul to resign from my position with the Consulate.

BARBARA: DON'T BE FOOLISH. I will ignore what you have said. I insist you take two weeks off with pay, return home, consider the situation.

CLAIRE: Thank you, I would do so, were you to consider for that time, allowing me to continue in my capacity as—

BARBARA: No. It would constitute a security risk to do so. My offer stands.

CLAIRE: Respectfully, Madam Consul, I, with great regret, resign my position.

Silence.

BARBARA: Good day, Ms. Hopkins, and good luck to you. While your decision is principled, I think it is made in the heat of one form of passion or another and thus is not weighed properly against the heavy counterbalance of contemporary realities. I offer you this one last chance to change your course.

CLAIRE: Thank you, Madam Consul for your good wishes,

I wish you, also, the very best.

BARBARA: We will send you your personal effects from your office by courier. *(She exits as this continues.)* We will need all keys, passes and consular I.D. from you immediately, as well as your business cards and any consular material you may have in your possession personally or in your home…

Scene Eleven

Evening. The airport, interrogation room.

MO: If I were to sign that document, it would be an admission of sorts…

JENKINS: Not exactly…

MO: It states clearly, that I understand that I am a security risk. It's very close to an admission of guilt.

JENKINS: What it states, I could read it again for you, is that you understand the security concerns that we have been discussing with you, that you share our concern vis a vis the safety of citizens of the United States of America, and that you are willingly identifying yourself as someone that we might consider to be a security risk. *(Short Pause.)* That's not an admission of guilt.

MO: You want me to agree…I cannot remember when last I slept or ate…

JENKINS: Let's finish this up, I can have a steak brought in, a beer, anything you like…

MO: You'd like me to sign this document which states that I understand that you might consider me a security risk…

JENKINS: Yes.

MO: How is this going to help either of us, in this situation.

JENKINS: Look, it's a start. That's all. If you like we can put in a clause that says for the present, that you admit no guilt, nor any association with any terrorist group.

MO: Admit no guilt? I haven't been charged yet, how could I admit guilt.

JENKINS: Exactly.

MO: It doesn't make sense.

JENKINS: It's paperwork. If you help us do our job, things will go better for you. A good steak, they have nice meat in the lounge, we'll have it brought in, a baked potato, butter… Do you eat regular meat? A beer?

MO: A steak would be good. No beer thank you. I've told you, I am not a practising Muslim…

JENKINS: Let's not get all that started again…OK?

JENKINS: Sign. Just sign. *(Pause.)* I'll call for the meal.

MO: No, look. How can I expect to get out of here, to be seen as someone innocent if I sign something that says I am willingly identifying myself as a security risk.

JENKINS: It could go a long way toward getting you home…

MO: Then what? I won't be able to work, I won't be able to come into the States again.

JENKINS: No. That's not necessarily so. You've not been in front of a judge. You're not yet facing a charge. I could show this to my boss, see. Show him I've got a cooperative guy down here. He sees that, he might understand… For sure he's not gonna let you go without it.

MO: But with it?

JENKINS: Well, that's another story. Whole other world of possibilities…see?

MO: Because I would be seen to be cooperating.

JENKINS: Exactly. *(Pause.)* Look, I can see what you are, who you are. You're a hard working guy, okay? That's evident. But you're not an average Joe, OK. Smart is what you are, hydrogen technology— Now that makes you stand out. Just that. Then there's the question of background, your father's family. So when it all adds up, it's let's face it. It's not the average profile. It's something else.

MO: …Suspicious.

JENKINS: So—you signing that, you looking at our point of view and saying just, not that you're guilty, saying how you could see how we might look at you as a security risk, that's a way to be rid of some of that suspicion.

MO: How?

JENKINS: It's a way to share a point of view. To get on the same page regarding that one thing. I mean look at it Mr. El Rafi. *(Pause.)* Look at it; your eyes can't sign it.

MO: I'm not ready to sign this…I would like to see the attorney from the Consul.

JENKINS: …They're in the process of assigning someone new, it could take a few days.

MO: Why someone new. What's happened to Ms. Hopkins?

JENKINS: She's no longer dealing with your case. Someone new has to be assigned to catch up on the situation etc. Bureaucracy, very slow...Canadians are as slow as the rest of us, if not slower, ha ha.

MO: Ms. Hopkins will not be back?

JENKINS: No.

MO: ...If I were to sign this it shows...

JENKINS: Willingness to cooperate. Shows good faith.

MO: Might I be returned to Canada.

JENKINS: I don't want to promise you that. That would be unwise for me. I don't want your hopes up, we're not there yet. I can promise you the steak, ice cream, a good salad if you like that, some bread...

MO: Do they have whole wheat bread?

JENKINS: The brown stuff?

MO: *(Short pause.)* Yes.

JENKINS: I'm pretty sure they do. I've had it myself. Very tasty, little seeds in it...chewy. I like it.

MO: ...Could you read it to me again?

JENKINS: I, Mohammed El Rafi, understand the security concerns that the Port Authority has, and those which they have been discussing with me, I share these concerns vis a vis the safety of the citizens of the United States of America, and I am willingly identifying myself as someone that the Port Authority and the Department of Homeland Security might consider to be a security risk.

MO: I don't like it...

JENKINS: I wouldn't like it. OK? But it is a good way to get into the same book. Let's face it, that's necessary. This is a bad situation you're in, and it has been going on for some days...

MO: Could I have a shower? If I could have a hot shower and think about it for a few minutes I would feel more clear…

JENKINS: How's it look…? I came in here, what ten minutes ago? So I walk back out with this signed and hand it to my boss, I say here, he signed it, it's done. My boss says, let's get to work on getting this guy processed. We have other guys, right? This isn't a jail here. Or, I go out there, I say, OK, he needs to think about this, he wants a hot shower—does not know if he agrees completely with the stated case, would like to maybe make some amendments to the statement as written. You get my drift.

MO: *(Pause.)* Yes.

JENKINS: I mean right now, this minute my boss is watching, right? And what you want, I know all you want is to get back to Canada. I mean all this other stuff is what, legal mumbo jumbo. *(Pause.)* You want my opinion? *(Pause.)* You want to know what I think Mo, and I think I've got a good sense of you, of what you're about—a lot of integrity…yes? OK, my personal advice, the job I'm doing aside, show some empathy for the people you're dealing with, for the country you came to on business… *(He draws a breath.)*

MO: And…?

JENKINS: …Sign the fucking paper.

MO: Sign it?

JENKINS: YES.

MO: …Now.

JENKINS: Yes.

MO: Yes, you're right…give it to me…

JENKINS: That's right, get it over with. It doesn't say much... here.

MO: OK, that's it. Alright, done.

JENKINS: Attaboy. Look, this is going to help. This is going to do things for you.

MO: I hope so.

JENKINS: Here, two more copies, same thing.

MO: Fine.

JENKINS: They say the same thing, read them if you like.

MO: I trust you.

JENKINS: I'm taking this straight to my boss, I'm gonna make a case for you.

MO: To get me outa here?

JENKINS: Sure, that's it. First, I'm gonna see to it you get that dinner we discussed. You like sour cream?

MO: *(Breaking down.)* Please, take the paper away, I feel sick to my stomach.

JENKINS: Mo. *(Pause.)* You did a good thing here. Don't feel bad. You did right.

JENKINS exits the room and we hear on the P.A. system the following:

Homeland Security in compliance with the Patriot Act reminds you: Freedom isn't free. Our precious freedom has a price. And sometimes the price of freedom is freedom itself.

Scene Twelve

Afternoon, a Saturday. The home of the El Rafi family. A quiet suburban cul de sac, birdsong.

CLAIRE: Mrs. El Rafi.

LAILA: You are?

CLAIRE: Claire Hopkins.

LAILA: Ms. Hopkins, I'm not interested in speaking with you…

CLAIRE: Please, Mrs. El Rafi, please, just a couple of moments of your time…I promised your husband… I'm on your side… I promised…

LAILA: The Consulate in New York told me that you are no longer working with them, that you resigned from your position…

CLAIRE: That's correct. I did resign…

LAILA: Then what possible use would it be to speak with you? I do not wish to worsen my husband's situation.

CLAIRE: I believe your husband is in great danger of being sent to Syria. I flew here to tell you this. I'm here to help—

LAILA: *(Pause.)* Come in, it's not illegal for me to speak with you is it?

The two women cross the threshold into private space.

CLAIRE: No. We're speaking as two individuals.

LAILA: Come in. My children are playing downstairs, they may come in, please don't speak of my husband being held if they are here…

CLAIRE: *(Short pause.)* I understand. I resigned from my position when I was told I could no longer look after your husband's case…

LAILA: Why did they not want you to look after my husband?

CLAIRE: *(Pause.)* They did not… *(Pause.)* I'm telling you this confidentially, you understand? It was suggested I was taking his case personally, forming too strong a personal connection. An attraction.

LAILA: …And?

CLAIRE: I am personally concerned for your husband. Every time I spoke with him his thoughts were for you and your children. He loves you very much, and asked me repeatedly to tell you so.

LAILA: …You have seen my husband, you have spent time with him. Excuse me, the stress, it's been now four, almost five days with him gone. He's not the political type…he works all day and night, he doesn't read the paper most days.

CLAIRE: I would like to help you, and to try to help your husband.

LAILA: I've had very little news from the Consulate.

CLAIRE: I would like to work for you, to try to resolve your husband's situation.

LAILA: How do we go about this?

CLAIRE: There's a lot of paperwork… But, basically it's a fight. *(Pause.)* What kind of work do you do?

LAILA: Just now, I'm at home with our kids. I was a teacher, I will go back to that in some time.

CLAIRE: You're comfortable speaking in front of groups.

LAILA: Groups of children, yes. I manage.

CLAIRE: Do you think you could speak in front of reporters?

LAILA: For my husband, yes. *(Pause.)* I could speak in front of a hurricane.

CLAIRE: That might be useful, there can be a lot of wind in the media…

LAILA: Where is he now, Claire? Right now.

CLAIRE: I'm not sure.

LAILA: Do you think he's still in New York?

CLAIRE: Perhaps, but I'm almost certain he will be sent to Syria if we don't have the intervention of our government in his case. Are you willing to work with me?

LAILA: Yes. We don't have unlimited resources…my husband will not be paid if he's not at work. I'm not sure how long we will make it without pay.

CLAIRE: You can pay me when you're able. I will need to get some other work as well…

LAILA: You are a kind person, I can see that.

CLAIRE: I'm self-interested. I don't like what's going on in my country. If I don't do something… *(Pause.)* My grandfather was in the Second World War. Dieppe. He used to wake up screaming sometimes at our cottage, everyone knew to stay in bed. Even the neighbours. My Gran woke up and made him mug after mug of hot cocoa. Then he wouldn't speak a word for two days. He'd be fishing quietly by the shore and you knew to leave him alone. The look on his face…the look. Like he'd done something wrong. *(Pause.)* I asked him once, what made him feel bad—when I was a teenager—breaking rules. He looked right through me and turned away. *(Pause.)* He had seven nine-millimetre shells go through various places on his body…his arms and legs mostly. It was a miracle he lived. And when he smiled you'd know that he meant it. Not like today's smiles. Negotiations, not smiles.

LAILA: You're talking about Canada; Mo is in America.

CLAIRE: Yes, and we're, "we" the country, we're looking the other way as regards his rights, it's a less attractive part of our national hertiage.

LAILA: *(Ironically.)* Is that a fact?

CLAIRE: That is, very much, categorically, a fact.

LAILA: *(Short pause.)* Where do we start?

Scene Thirteen

Evening, the airport, interrogation room, Port Authority, Customs.

JENKINS: Here get started on this, it's still hot. Look, I kept a cover on it, keep it warm.

MO: Thank you.

JENKINS: Smells good…?

MO: Yes.

JENKINS: Go ahead, I had dinner.

MO: What time is it?

JENKINS: Seven p.m. I had to cut it up for you, I can't give you a steak knife.

MO: *(Eating.)* Very good.

JENKINS: You like it?

MO: Yes, I am hungry, at this point anything…but yes it is good.

JENKINS: I know the waiter, I told him get me a special steak, a really good one, VIP in our area.

MO: You did?

JENKINS: Yeah why not?

MO and JENKINS laugh together on this.

MO: VIP?

JENKINS: That's what I told him.

MO: What I signed, the paper…?

JENKINS: Yeah…?

MO: It…it…what did your boss say?

JENKINS: First, eat your steak.

MO: It's good; I am.

Silence, except for eating.

What did he say?

JENKINS: I don't want to spoil your dinner.

MO: *(Pause.)* That doesn't sound good.

JENKINS: Do you eat all of one thing first and then the other?

MO: You mean…like the potato last?

JENKINS: Yeah.

MO: I have a confession for you.

JENKINS: Yes?

MO: Truly.

JENKINS: Go on.

MO: I do eat the potato last. I eat the steak, then the vegetables, then last the potato.

JENKINS: I thought that was an Irish thing. That's what the men do in my family…

MO: There's Irish in my mother's side.

JENKINS: There is?

MO: Yes. Farmers, Northern Ontario.

JENKINS: I'll be…

MO: Yeah.

JENKINS: I thought you were Middle Eastern, through and through.

MO: Perhaps from the waist up, or perhaps from the waist down…

JENKINS: …I've got bad news for you Mo, top and bottom.

MO: …yes?

JENKINS: My boss was happy with what you signed, well happy…he felt it was a step in the right direction…

MO: …Yes.

JENKINS: He wants more.

MO: What more can I say.

JENKINS: That's it, he feels we haven't had enough from you, not enough of substance.

MO: I don't know much that's of use outside of my field.

JENKINS: He's going to make a case to his higher ups, he believes what you say about not knowing more…

MO: Does he?

JENKINS: He does, he believes, my boss believes you're very credible he says—

MO: So, what's the matter then?

JENKINS: *(Pause.)* It may be that we will have some incriminating evidence coming from your RCMP and CSIS.

MO: There's nothing that can incriminate me, I am innocent.

JENKINS: Do you remember having coffee the 5th of November last year on Saint Laurent, in Montreal?

MO: Not specifically, no.

JENKINS: Think on that, think on that hard. Once the information is here, once we've received it, it's seen very differently from your volunterring it… Think on it, the 5th of November…

MO: …Sometimes I meet a second cousin for coffee.

JENKINS: Think on it. My boss is going to make a case to his boss, saying it's not needed, but the brass, they think you need to go to Syria. *(Silence.)* I'm working to prevent that. I'm working with you.

MO: …I signed the paper.

JENKINS: It helped, believe me, it helped. If you hadn't signed that paper, this very minute you'd be flying over the Atlantic…

MO: I signed.

JENKINS: My boss wants to be able to make a case to his superiors…the RCMP file isn't going to help you, can you tell us who might have been in the coffee shop the 5th of November?

MO: Look, I told you—whatever you need from me, OK? I'm not a soldier, I'm not an extremist. Tell me what it is and I'll say it...but I can't tell you who was in a coffee shop...I'm not a clairvoyant—

JENKINS: My boss wants you to sign a document saying that you're not afraid to go to Syria to be interrogated there.

MO: ...Why would I sign that?

JENKINS: It would go a long way to show the brass that... well, how serious you are.

MO: *(Pause.)* Give me the paper.

JENKINS: *(Pause.)* OK, I have copy right here.

JENKINS reaches into his jacket's breast pocket.

MO: I'll bet you do.

MO continues to eat.

Get a pen.

JENKINS: Here.

MO: ...Sign this before my potatoes get cold. OK? There, done.

JENKINS: Terrific.

MO: Done. Satisfied?

JENKINS: Yes. This is good. My boss can take this to his supervisor...then as a—

MO: Good.

JENKINS: You don't want to hear...?

MO: I don't believe it. Since I've been here...normally it would be your job, to test my credibility to see if I'm believable...

JENKINS: Yes.

MO: That's not what you've done. You had an idea of me when first I came into your custody and it has not changed…I fit the profile and that's it. It doesn't matter if I argue, it doesn't matter what I say. You know what you're going to decide. So why lose energy? You have your form, OK?

JENKINS: I didn't know you were part Irish.

MO: But apart from that, I fit the profile and that's it.

JENKINS: It's not me. It's the higher ups…

MO: Fine. Now they have a signed lie.

JENKINS: A lie?

MO: It is a lie that I'm not afraid to go to Syria, and you need this, why? Legal reasons. Court of law, after all the beatings are done, and I'm quite possibly dead. "Look your honour, he wasn't afraid of being shipped there." For all I know, that document gives you permission to ship me there.

JENKINS: Pretty damn close. But the fact is we don't need your permission, we can ship you there anytime we want. 'Cause you're our detainee, and a suspected illegal combatant…

MO: Yes, yes, yes…

JENKINS: So if you have anything, anything at all that might help get us off this track of send Mo to Syria…

MO: I haven't anything. Understand. I have nothing for you. It's not resistance. DIDN'T YOU SEE ME SIGN THAT FORM? I HAVE NO RESISTANCE.

JENKINS: *(Pause.)* OK.

MO: So now what?

JENKINS: I'll show this to my boss, make a case.

MO: I'm finished.

JENKINS: Yeah?

MO: I'm done my potatoes.

JENKINS: Alright.

Scene Fourteen

Daytime. Airport in Ottawa.

JOHNSTON: You understand, though? The situation?

LAILA: I understand what you're telling me. I don't agree with it.

JOHNSTON: Would you like me to repeat it—?

CLAIRE: I'm not sure that would help, Mr. Johnston…

JOHNSTON: My time is short, I have a flight to catch, back to New York. This meeting is a courtesy to both of you…

LAILA: Courtesy? You consider it a courtesy to tell me that our government has stood by while my husband was kidnapped…

JOHNSTON: Please, kidnapped, please. Let's not…

CLAIRE: Damn close to it, what else would you call it?

JOHNSTON: Deported.

CLAIRE: One is normally deported to one's country of citizenship.

JOHNSTON: One is not assured of such courtesy in our current climate.

LAILA: "One" who is of Middle Eastern extraction.

JOHNSTON: One might say that. I did not.

CLAIRE: We're not recording you, speak frankly, please.

JOHNSTON: I am speaking frankly…

LAILA: This would not be happening if Mo had not been born in Syria, would it?

JOHNSTON: I can't verify the veracity of that, but he was born in Syria.

CLAIRE: Citizenship, not national origin is what matters here, it's a constitutional guarantee, a charter right.

JOHNSTON: …INSIDE OUR COUNTRY, YES.

LAILA: Mr. Johnston, Claire, please…Mo is…he's not a terrorist.

JOHNSTON: The entire West is in a state of high alert, no one knows what's next…

CLAIRE: Canada's not at war.

JOHNSTON: It doesn't much matter, nor do formal declarations versus actual facts. The atmosphere is one of war… how many times can we in the West be attacked without thinking war?

LAILA: Has it occured to you that Muslim countries might be thinking in just such a way…?

JOHNSTON: That's a lengthy debate—which I have neither the time nor the authority to entertain. *(Pause.)* Who knows what could be next, an attack on Canadian soil? Everyone imagines themselves a possible victim…and they look for someone to blame…

LAILA: Mr. Johnston; this I can't argue with, I feel it. I'm not naïve. *(Pause.)* I feel people looking at me differently than ever before in my life and I was born here…

JOHNSTON: I'm sorry to hear that…

Pause.

CLAIRE: What?

JOHNSTON: I'm sorry that's your experience…

CLAIRE gives JOHNSTON a hard look.

LAILA: …I've never had so much attention, eyes on the back of my neck all the time, till it's hot, and people staring at my handbag, my shopping bags…I don't even dare to have a nail clipper in my bag…

JOHNSTON: I'm very sorry, Mrs. El Rafi…

CLAIRE: Mr. Johnston, you don't look very sorry.

JOHNSTON: *(Pause.)* If an undertaker wept every time someone died, there'd be no one left to comfort the living. *(Pause.)* I'm not happy to hear that people look at you in an odd manner.

LAILA: This, I'm used to. But to have my husband, an engineer, a father, a decent, kind man, kidnapped…

JOHNSTON: I'm not sure kidnapping is the best way to—

CLAIRE: What would you call it?

JOHNSTON: *(Pause.)* Repatriated to one's country of birth.

CLAIRE: Is that an official phrase, or did you just come up with that?

JOHNSTON: I have apologized, I've given you all the information I have, I have agreed to work with you to the best of my ability from my office in New York; you will need to establish contact with the appropriate people here in Ottawa, my secretary—

LAILA: The appropriate people—by that do you mean the government, or the Department of Foreign Affairs…?

JOHNSTON: The Department—

LAILA: And the government, what's their position on this…?

JOHNSTON: The government has not taken a position—

LAILA: That sounds so effortless…so disconnected from you.

JOHNSTON: I'm not the government Mrs. El Rafi…

LAILA: You work for the government…

JOHNSTON: Yes, within a Department for another week or so… The government, if you mean by that Parliament, the politicians; that is specifically what I am not. As an employee of Foreign Affairs, I work as an instrument effecting departmental policy as set by the Minister and Federal Cabinet, etc.

Pause.

CLAIRE: Which is a nice bureaucratic way of saying, that it's not his fault.

LAILA: So what does the Minister have to say, or the Prime Minister?

JOHNSTON: So far they have said nothing; as far as I know neither has any specific knowledge of the case. And they have been kept in the dark—

LAILA: So who will bring this to the government's attention?

JOHNSTON: It's a good question. I've filed my reports, Claire spoke with the Consul, resigned, may be at risk for continuing to be involved…

CLAIRE: Mr. Johnston, given that the department is not doing anything and that neither the Minister nor Prime Minister have intervened…

JOHNSTON: …Yes.

LAILA: Whose job is it to bring this to the attention of the government?

Pause.

JOHNSTON: You might go to your Member of Parliament. *(Pause.)* Ultimately, that falls to the individual's family.

LAILA: To me?

JOHNSTON: Yes.

CLAIRE: Now that it's likely Mr. El Rafi is to be deported, we would very much like to know what the department is prepared to do for him.

JOHNSTON: We'll keep you up to date on any developments. That's all I can promise for now…

CLAIRE: So the government in total is washing its hands of this man? They are not defending the normal convention of deportation to the country of one's current citizenship?

JOHNSTON: Our government can only govern inside its borders. It can't decide matters for the United States.

LAILA: Can you tell me one last thing…?

JOHNSTON: I've told you everything that I know…

LAILA: Why? Why Mohammed? Why a man who has never…?

JOHNSTON: Why Mohammed? *(Pause.)* You want to know why?

CLAIRE: *(Not liking this direction.)* Thank you Mr. Johnston, we've taken too much of your time already…

JOHNSTON: Because someone has got to pay. Failing that, someone has got to be seen to be paying.

LAILA: Are you serious?

JOHNSTON: You asked…

CLAIRE: Laila, we're done, let's go…

LAILA: I want to hear this…

JOHNSTON: This is not Johnston the bureaucrat speaking, the man with forty-odd years in the job; this is me personally telling you why, since you asked…

CLAIRE: We need to end this…

JOHNSTON: The terrorists, the actual terrorists are in hiding, they're fanatic but not stupid, they're not likely flying into New York on actual papers, not living under actual identities. But until they can be found, or curbed, yes you will feel eyes on the back of your neck, and yes you will think twice about carrying a nail clipper, and yes people will stand barefoot in airports and have their personal things husked like so much corn; and occasionally feel a probing finger, sheathed in a rubber glove… But you, you in particular, and people like you, which is to say, all people of Middle Eastern extraction will pay the price…

CLAIRE: Mr. Johnston, this is inappropriate, are you quite finished?

LAILA: Let him speak Claire, it's good to hear someone speak their mind, I can see it on a hundred faces a week…

JOHNSTON: …this is the price of having broken our ideals, of having set us against ourselves. So you have my apologies Mrs. El Rafi, as an employee of Foreign Affairs Canada, and as a private person. As a man on the street, retired as of Monday next, you also have my deep and abiding suspicion, as does your husband. *(Pause.)* It's human nature, even in a pluralistic, liberal, democratic society.

Pause.

LAILA: Most people are unwilling to say as much. I thank you for your candour, even though I disagree with your conclusions as to the normal functioning of a democracy…

CLAIRE: Thank you for meeting with us, Mr. Johnston.

Pause.

JOHNSTON: Well ladies, as they say in Québec, "Adieu."

Scene Fifteen

Night. MO and JENKINS aboard a small jet plane.

JENKINS: "Every Opportunity." That's what my higher ups call it.

MO: …That's what you call it?

JENKINS: Yes.

MO: Don't you think if I had something I could have told you—

JENKINS: If you did have something that you were hiding, you would resist as long as possible.

MO: Come on, you're kidding. You don't believe that.

JENKINS: "Absolute Certainty", that's the goal of interrogation. Can I be absolutely certain of your claimed innocence? No.

MO: This is philosophy, reduced to aphorisms.

JENKINS: *(Sarcastically.)* Let me get that down, I need something in my notes.

MO: Aphorisms. A-P-H-O-R—

JENKINS: —isms right? I can handle the rest… You have a pretty developed vocabulary.

MO: For a primitive tribesman?

JENKINS: For an illegal combatant. I personally don't think they've got the right guy here.

MO: …Don't, please don't . Whenever you cosy up to me, my situation is in imminent danger of worsening.

JENKINS: Well, I'm calling it as I see it.

MO: …Don't, OK.

JENKINS: Alright… Do you need anything?

MO: Can you get these handcuffs taken off me?

JENKINS: Not while we're in flight.

Short silence.

MO: What are you afraid of?

Pause.

JENKINS: Fanatics.

Long pause. MO just stares at JENKINS.

What? *(Pause.)* What?

MO: No comment. Put it in your notes. No comment.

JENKINS: Are you implying something.

MO: Yes, with absolute certainty, I am. At every opportunity.

JENKINS: What's that supposed to mean, huh?

MO: *(Quietly.)* Nothing.

JENKINS: For my notes, what's it mean? Don't be ambiguous, it can read the wrong way. Especially in a typed transcript of a recorded conversation, without the tone of voice…

MO: Those are your phrases, I have no idea what they mean to you.

JENKINS: And where did you hear them; from where did you gain knowledge of these phrases?

MO: *(As though for a microphone.)* From an agent named Jenkins, sitting beside me in a small jet aircraft.

JENKINS: Thank you, the recording was not up till we had exchanged more than a few words.

MO: I'll bear that in mind, a couple of pleasantries to get the gear rolling. May I ask you here formally, while we are being monitored, what evidence, if any, you have against me?

JENKINS: Yes. Our great leader says "In this war you can tell if a man is guilty by where he stands. If he's in front of you, he's guilty."

MO: So I have no chance then?

JENKINS: All you have to do is tell us things, things that are useful… we are giving you every opportunity.

MO: There it is again, what do you mean by that?

JENKINS: It's protocol, suspects should be given every opportunity to divulge information before moving from stress and duress to the infliction of pain and more extreme forms of interrogation…

MO: Why are you deliberately frightening me?

JENKINS: I'm telling you the facts. The facts of your situation.

MO: You're suggesting that I will be tortured?

JENKINS: Right now we're in American airspace. I can tell you no such thing. Once we are outside of American airspace, we're in a whole other world. Once you're in Syria, you will be buried in shit.

MO: …I'm aware of that, don't you think that would be sufficient to get me to tell you of anything I know of.

JENKINS: Every opportunity, that's what we're giving you now. Right now.

MO: Before moving onto guaranteeing "Absolute Certainty"?

JENKINS: …That's it.

MO: Which will be achieved through torture?

JENKINS: Stop with that, you're going to scare yourself to death.

MO: I am scared to death…

JENKINS: You don't show it.

MO: You don't know me, what's your benchmark?

JENKINS: Certain indicators in blood pressure and pulse?

MO: *(He looks around him to see where this information could be coming from.)* Which you have an idea of from?

JENKINS: Never you fucking mind…

Short pause.

MO: Temper, temper.

JENKINS: I'm getting tired of this…

MO: …You're getting tired?

JENKINS: You're too smart, too smart by half to be a credible suspect for a fanatic. But you've rung certain bells, you've hit certain sensors.

MO: Which are?

JENKINS: Again, never you fucking mind.

MO: Is that an official position?

JENKINS: Yes.

MO: I can put that in my notes?

JENKINS: What notes?

MO: Mentally, I'm taking notes mentally.

JENKINS: Who's interrogating who here?

MO: You're quite right.

JENKINS: *(Suddenly grabbing MO.)* Don't condescend to me. *(Short pause.)* That's something you Canadians kept from the Brits, that condescension when you don't agree…

MO: Are you acknowledging me as being Canadian?

JENKINS: You've lived a good part of your life in Canada, but where you were born is the main thing…

MO: Are you absolutely certain that what you are doing is the right thing? Can you not see that someone reviewing your case, might say you had every opportunity to find me clear of wrongdoing? That someone reviewing what you are currently doing might find you guilty of a war crime, and might find that you had broken numerous laws and international coventions such as the Geneva Convention… Can you be absolutely certain that you will not one day be seen as a war criminal who had every opportunity…?

Silence, the two men staring at each other.

JENKINS: We'll see…soon enough. Not here, not now.

Silence.

What are you thinking?

MO: Private thoughts.

JENKINS: Such as.

MO: *(Pause.)* Things which are private.

JENKINS: I keep trying to give you…

MO & JENKINS: …every opportunity.

JENKINS: That's right. *(As though dropping all pretense.)* I've been on your side, since the start. I don't think they've got the right guy. *(Pause.)* So just tell me, what were you thinking.

MO: …My son has a soccer game this weekend, I was supposed to drive certain of the kids…

JENKINS: Like I said, we've got the wrong guy. What's your son's name?

MO: Ahmed, he goes by Ed with his friends.

JENKINS: …He is what age?

MO: …Twelve.

JENKINS: …Has he or any of his friends demonstrated interest in Jihad…or terrorist type activities and interests.

MO: He's twelve…

JENKINS: His interests are?

MO: Soccer.

JENKINS: And?

MO: Chocolate ice cream…

The sound of flight from the interior of the small jet rises, as lights go out then rise on the next scene.

Scene Sixteen

Afternoon, outside the Press Club, Ottawa.

LAILA: In the case of my husband and others like him, the Canadian government, starting with the office of the Prime Minister and continuing down through the ranks has adopted the position of a well known old fashioned knick knack. We all know the three brass monkeys: "see no evil, hear no evil, speak no evil." While this is a charming idea in a china cabinet, we do expect more from our government. I am a Canadian citizen, my husband is a Canadian citizen, we want our rights as citizens, nothing more, nothing less. My husband, Mohammed El Rafi is currently being detained in Syria. I ask the Canadian government to become more involved, deal with my lawyer Ms. Claire Hopkins, deal with me—show us some evidence or charges against my husband or work with us to free him. This is the job of our government. I can only imagine for those of you listening you would insist upon the same for your husband or wife, brother, sister or fellow citizen. Thank you.

Scene Seventeen

In dim light, a sedated MO is placed in a hole not much larger than a grave, made of what appears to be concrete. (Ideally, a deep trap in the stage floor.) Lights rise indicating passage of time—then fall, rise and fall again. In darkness, as though night-time, two guards appear and stand over the cell, they urinate at length into the cell as though it were routine. The guards then take an extra heavy duty charging cable and hook it up to a set of metal bars that covers the hole. One stands back a distance, the other goes a large old fashioned bus bar type circuit breaker switch and opens it. Current is seen on the contacts. A white-blue light emanates from the cell and we hear MO screaming.

Scene Eighteen

Night. In MO's cell, two days after arriving in Syria.

JENKINS: This is bad, very very bad. *(He places a hand on MO.)*

MO: DON'T TOUCH ME, DON'T…

JENKINS: I want to see if you're alright. See if you have any broken bones…

MO: …They don't need to break bones…

JENKINS: It's been a couple of days, have you had any food?

MO: Don't take that tone with me—

JENKINS: —What?

MO: Don't talk nicely to me—

JENKINS: Why not?

MO: You did this to me, you put me here. You personally— and your government.

JENKINS: I did not do that to you. That was done by your people, your government; not me, not mine.

MO: These are not my—these animals are acting on your behalf, regardless of where they were born or who they otherwise are. *(Pause.)* Note it down, put it in your file.

JENKINS: I didn't see anything—but I heard, I know what they—

MO: LOOK… *(He pulls up his shirt revealing heavy bruising.)*

You heard me confess to being places, I've never been, seeing people I've never seen, doing things I've never done. Do you have your absolute certainty now?

JENKINS: We mighta got the wrong guy. *(Short pause.)* Either way, it's too late.

Scene Nineteen

Afternoon, LAILA's home.

CLAIRE: We are getting somewhere… The Minister is communicating with me directly…

LAILA: Through his assistant. Communicating with you…

CLAIRE: They feel more comfortable speaking with a lawyer… We need to back off, for a little while. That's what I've been told.

LAILA: They told you that?

CLAIRE: We have to tust our government; trust is a tenet of a free society.

LAILA: You hear from someone who's heard from someone, from someone else on the other side of the world—and I hear from you.

CLAIRE: What we are hearing is good…however they say we may be placing Mohammed at risk by causing an embarrassment to both governments.

LAILA: Embarrassment!? *(Short pause.)* The embarrassment is that the man, my husband is being held, has been held these last nine months without having been charged…with no evidence, no charges…

CLAIRE: It's outrageous, I agree, but if we were to back off just a little at this point we might have some goodwill build on our side.

LAILA: Claire, it's been nine months, I could have had a child in his absence, had I been pregnant…

CLAIRE: As long as we are front page, it presents a thorn in the side for the Syrian government especially, here too, it doesn't help.

LAILA: I disagree, vehemently I disagree.

CLAIRE: Yes, but—

LAILA: Claire, listen to me. I've taken your advice in every instance, we've never disagreed, to this point have we?

CLAIRE: No, we haven't.

LAILA: Understand then, that I will not move one millimetre. What I am doing, what we are doing is not illegal. It is not immoral. We cannot be faulted for keeping Mohammed's case in the papers, on TV.

CLAIRE: …Except that on a diplomatic level…

LAILA: On a diplomatic level they've got Mo in detention, somewhere indeterminate, somewhere who knows where, in Syria…

CLAIRE: …Yes…

LAILA: You yourself have said repeatedly this is contrary…a violation in fact of custom and international—

CLAIRE: Nothing in my position has changed…it's a question of breathing room, when for example an animal is in a corner…

LAILA: Do you believe that we, you and I have our government and the government of Syria in a corner?

CLAIRE: Yes, in a manner of speaking.

LAILA: *(Laughing.)* Incredible…

CLAIRE: They can't be seen to be bowing to public pressure. Both governments…otherwise every time…

LAILA: Every time someone is illegally detained there might be a cry from the public?

CLAIRE: Yes, I suppose…what I want—

LAILA: I don't accept that.

CLAIRE: It's meant to be a representational democracy, not run by public sentiment per se.

LAILA: I'm not asking to run the government…

CLAIRE: So they don't want for it to seem like the public has decided…

LAILA: I don't sleep much as it is; I could not close my eyes or even so much as lie on a bed if I did not feel that every day, at the end of every day, I had done my best, my utmost for Mo. I sometimes feel as though I am digging to China alone in this.

CLAIRE: Alone?

LAILA: You know what I mean…

CLAIRE: Tell me…

LAILA: …You are involved, and I appreciate your commitment, your generosity—I have lost—

CLAIRE: I cannot compete with that, Laila, nor dare I to. What is being lost here, along with Mo, is our society, my liberty, the ideals I was raised on…our Charter Of Rights…

LAILA: So why would we back off? Freedoms cannot exist only when it is convenient. That's not freedom, it's a leash with a choke collar… What was it you called it, in law, when normal liberties are suspended, a state of exception?

CLAIRE: Yes…

LAILA: Can we have an ongoing state of exception in a democracy? *(Pause.)* Guaranteed rights and freedoms under a charter that might be seen at any time as inconvenient…that are then indefinitely suspended; both things at once…?

CLAIRE: We see this the same way, it's politeness I am talking about to back off just a little…I promised to bring it up with you, and nothing more…

LAILA: *(Pause.)* You promised them?

CLAIRE: Off the record; to discuss this with you. If as they say, they think a diplomatic solution is within reach, and if we could simply take a slightly lower profile…

LAILA: …We do not know his whereabouts or condition…

CLAIRE: It's been nine months, you said it yourself. When do you think would be an appropriate time to reevalute our strategy? *(Pause.)* What I want is to get Mo out—at any price. We can restate our case when he's safely home. We have to trust them.

LAILA: *(Pause.)* Claire, this is the last time I will say it, I will not back off, I will not, I will not. I'm out of trust.

Silence.

CLAIRE: So be it. We will not back off.

Scene Twenty

MO, speaking to LAILA, seated at their dining room table. He speaks as though speaking to LAILA, though he cannot see her, even though she is sitting at the table with him. Perhaps at the end of the speech he appears to see her and speaks directly to her.

MO: My dearest wife, having no paper and no pen, I am writing you on a piece of black slate which I have found on the inside of my mind, with a piece of white chalk extruded from my heart. How much we take for granted in times of peace. How lost we become in a struggle for prosperity. How far we travel from our own selves and each other. I feel I have not seen you in years. Some part of that is from this current situation, some part from the pursuit of a job that left no time to spend with you and the children. *(Pause.)* The situation I am in is quite bad. My spirit is yet strong. I worry most for you and the children, how long will the savings last. I am being kept in a hole in the ground with bars over top, made of concrete, no plumbing, this would be a mean way to keep an animal. Not a cell or a jail, a place for the burial of the living, without the privacy of the earth falling in on you. But I am as yet intact. I know you will act for me, and try your best to do what can be done with our government. I had never thought of Canada in this way, as being so weak with its size and strength, but would be happiest ever, only to be home with you all. Having no post office, courier packs, email or fax machine to send this letter, I send it from my mind to your mind via the world of spirit, and with it I send all of the love I have and that which I receive from you. Rest assured, I know I am in your heart and thoughts constantly, and that I have hope and much desire to see you all again, soon. Love, Mo.

Scene Twenty-One

LAILA now speaking to MO, and still they are seated at their dining room table. She speaks as though speaking to MO, though she cannot see him even though he is sitting at the table with her. Again, perhaps at the end of the speech she seems to see him and speaks directly to him.

LAILA: Mo. My thoughts are with you constantly. These last months… I have worried so much, I cannot say. *(Pause.)* I sold my car, kept yours for the time being, the lease… Stopped the cable, cancelled magazines, stopped using aluminium foil, plastic wrap, prepared foods of any kind. Every penny is counted. I had your cell phone put on a minimal plan. I don't imagine you've had it for some time, but somehow I couldn't cancel it, in case you got it back. I hope they feed you. I hope you are treated alright.*(Pause.)* We read and talk more, the kids and I, we don't even rent videos. Your parents help, my parents help- The children don't ask for anything, can you imagine? Ahmed is growing fast, he has aches and pains he's growing so quickly. Maya is still very much a little girl. They ask a lot of questions…I tell them you will come home, that we must continue to hope. *(Pause.)* I wish I could reach out and touch you, and in my mind, I can; stroke your cheek with the back of my hand. Place my palm and fingers on your forehead. Hold you close and smell you, drink you in. *(Pause.)* You remember Ahmed's birth, how nervous you were, how jumpy. How you cried, Maya's birth, how proud, how helpful. You remember when we met at McGill, first kiss in the bandstand. You remember our parents' first meeting, everyone so nervous. You remember…you remember, me your wife, your home where you belong— It will return, it will all return, I promise you. I promise.

Scene Twenty-Two

Evening, LAILA's home.

CLAIRE: By the end of the week is what they said.

LAILA: Is that right—?

CLAIRE: I believe it Laila.

LAILA: You do?

CLAIRE: Foreign affairs wouldn't say "the end of the week" if they weren't sure of it.

Pause.

LAILA: All I want is to see Mo, put my hands on him, and know that he's OK…

CLAIRE: I understand.

LAILA: *(Pause.)* I can't tell you what I'll feel when Mo's back, I'll want to speak with him, spend some time…

CLAIRE: I understand.

LAILA: Then we need to continue this fight, the three of us. *(Pause.)* What if he just wants to get on with his life…

CLAIRE: I suppose that's possible—

LAILA: But until he clears his name, this will be his life…

CLAIRE: I believe so.

LAILA: He will want to see the situation addressed, he will want to right what's wrong.

CLAIRE: Do you want to keep working, after his return?

LAILA: The answer is yes. *(Pause.)* It has to be done.

CLAIRE: Yes? Are you sure you want to take on our government, the government of the United States, the U.S. State Department?

LAILA: Yes, yes of course yes…I just want him home.

CLAIRE: "By the end of the week."

Scene Twenty-Three

Morning. International Arrivals Area, Trudeau Airport.

MO enters upstage unsure of quite where he is. He moves down a corridor toward LAILA, they move toward one another as everyone else watches on. They embrace, hold and kiss one another, stroking one another's faces, they embrace again. As the above is happening a photographic flash goes off then another, then another until the action is in a slow strobing flash. MO slowly turns his head away from LAILA and lets out an anguished cry which turns into a roar, the roar is overtaken by the sound of people, mounting, and then mixed into the sound of a waterfall.

The End.

Acknowledgments

Thanks to The Canada Council for the Arts, CBC Radio, Dave Carley, Damiano Piettropaulo and the company, GCTC, Lorne Pardy, Arthur Milner, Michael Shamata, John Ferguson and the company, David Strathairn and Logan Goodman, the company of Arrivals at the Bank Street Theatre, NYC, and Stanley Bard at the Chelsea.

All of the interpretive artists, crew and company who worked so hard to tug and pull such a blueprint into three dimensions and hold it there fast for the view, scrutiny and we hope enjoyment of the public. Also my whole family for their constant encouragement and support (including, but not limited to): Martine Gow-Cooper, Andrew, Phillippe and Jeremy Gow, Gabriel Compton and Phil Baugniet, Robert and Phyllis Baugniet, Jay and Catherine Kalò and family, as well as longtime friends (including, but not limited to): Jacob Potashnik and family, Paula Potashnik, Bachar Chbib and family, Mollye Reisler, Thom Richardson, Vittorio Rossi, Alain Harvey and Claude Villeneuve, Tibi and Isabelle Marcotte, Mary Pearson, Hrothgar Mathews and family, Robin Mathews and Esther Mathews, Piero Hirsch and family, Robert Astle and family, Joseph Drapell and family, Anne and Josh Hellman, Jay Harris and family, and all those of you who do not see your name here, but reckon it should be. Finally for the book itself, Glenda MacFarlane and Gord Shillingford.